T0193523

THERE'S A

LONELY

ANT

CROSSING THE

VERANDA

THOMAS J.F

WESTBOW
PRESS®
A DIVISION OF THOMAS NELSON
& ZONDERVAN

The original version of *"Bruised Reeds"* by J. F. Thomas was
published as a devotion in the Christian Medical Journal
of India in 1996. It has been revised for this book.

WestBow Press books may be ordered through booksellers or by contacting:

WestBow Press
A Division of Thomas Nelson & Zondervan
1663 Liberty Drive
Bloomington, IN 47403
www.westbowpress.com
844-714-3454

ISBN: 978-1-6642-9470-7 (sc)
ISBN: 978-1-6642-9471-4 (e)

Library of Congress Control Number: 2023905035

Print information available on the last page.

WestBow Press rev. date: 03/20/2023

Contents

A majority of the chapters of this book were originally posted on my Facebook wall and subsequently revised and edited for inclusion in the book. The events and incidents mentioned in this book reflect real-life relationships, momentary and long standing. All the characters in the book have taught me significant and important life-transforming lessons. However, the names of characters have been changed, modified, or altered to protect their identities and privacy as required by law.

To my parents, who strove to inculcate lasting values in me. To all my teachers in the chapters of this book—formal, informal, occasional, and accidental.

Acknowledgement:
I thank my WestBow Press editor for
effective line editing and helpful advice.

Teacher Ant

The hospital where I was born was shut down due to a lack of resources. I had heard that the former principal of my medical college was restarting it. When vacancies were announced, I felt sentimental and applied for a job as a medical record officer. I was fortunate to get the job and had the responsibility of not only managing the medical record department but also assisting patient and doctor support services with the help of my staff. Soon Rachel managed to join the hospital as a librarian. It was while serving there that we had our 'Blessing of the Marriage' ceremony. The hospital organized a reception for us and another couple who got married around the same time, and it was truly a memorable celebration with choral singing, decorations, and dinner.

Rachel and I were married in May of 1985 but had to wait two years to start living together. We had a civil wedding due to certain family circumstances and emotional upheavals. Rachel lived in the nurses' hostel, while I lived in the humble staff quarters assigned to me. In the evenings, most of the staff visited my home to chitchat, and Rachel joined them. There was much fun and laughter. Ambur, where the hospital was located, was a small town. The recreational facilities in the town were few at the time, and that made us spend our evenings in that small one-bedroom unit.

My childhood friends visited us whenever possible. The visits of colleagues were so regular that the day after our return from our blessing, a troupe of young colleagues marched to our house in the evening as usual. They were all freshened up for the visit, and some had a generous layer of talcum powder on their faces, which glittered under the harsh evening sun. Hubert, our gregarious pharmacist fondly called Fat Cat, had the most layers, outshining the others. I saw them through the window and alerted Rachel that they were about to visit us. Just then, our neighbor, the hospital's accountant, stepped outside his house to stop them, asking if they did not realize that we were newly married and needed our personal space and time. I felt sorry for them as they reluctantly turned around and marched back.

During my first Christmas at the hospital, a young pharmacist named Antony approached me with a request to direct the Christmas play, and I agreed. The Christmas story turned elastic and had to be stretched on a daily basis, because more and more young colleagues wanted to be part of the cast. Some took responsibility for the props, while others volunteered to take care of costumes and makeup. We practiced sincerely for almost a month.

On the day of the show, one actor fell flat on his face after tripping over a cable, and the props person followed up with an equally nasty, unintended dive to the ground. Fortunately, there were no injuries or damage to the set. As director, I had to hold things together with desperate prayers. We decided to make the journey of the magi as realistic as possible; therefore, the props team hung a star on a cable tied between a tree and the stage. A light bulb inside the star was also connected. The star was supposed to slowly slide down the cable, from the tree to the stage. The magi were to follow the star. During rehearsal, it worked just fine, and all of us applauded the props team. The costumes and makeup team used brightly colored silk saris to make robes for the wise men. Once they were dressed with makeup on, they really looked like wise men, defying reality.

In the evening, the play started without major mishaps. I was backstage, prompting actors and getting more and more nervous with butterflies in my stomach. It was time for the wise men to visit baby Jesus. I could not see them, as I was behind a screen, keeping my fingers crossed and praying. I heard some tittering and peeped out to see that the star, which had worked fine during the rehearsal, had gotten stuck midway down the cable. Before I could recover from the shock, there was a roar of laughter from the audience; the reason for their hilarity was that one of the wise men was showing off his new wristwatch. By the time the play reached its climax, it had almost turned into a crime thriller. We had a real newborn baby as the infant Jesus with the consent of his Muslim mother, who was only too happy. When the baby was about to be handed over to old Simeon by Mary and Joseph, the actor almost dropped the baby, and the audience gasped in horror. Needless to say, I almost had a heart attack and only recovered when I heard the audience's roaring applause at the end.

We, the staff of the hospital were certainly a team. The director, who was fondly called *Mama* (meaning *uncle* in Tamil) behind his back, made sure that the stifling health professional hierarchy was limited to professional practice. Once a working day was over, we spent time together, playing ball badminton, and during weekends, we watched TV in the director's house. Some of the doctors made a beeline to our humble staff quarters almost daily to borrow books from us and, when on night duty, to have the spice-flavored tea that I used to make. We were all truly a community of caring equals.

It was there that Rachel conceived and had a difficult pregnancy with repeated attacks of bronchial asthma. She was put on steroids almost throughout the entire pregnancy. My mother and sister came down to support us close to the due date. When Rachel went into labor, the hospital referred her to our alma mater, which is a teaching hospital fifty-five kilometers away.

We rushed her there, and she had to undergo a caesarian section to deliver Abishek. Because of Rachel's case history and the baby's sugar levels, Abishek was sent to the pediatric ICU right after delivery. Considering Rachel's health, her parents came to support us after her discharge from the hospital, and thereafter my mother and sister offered to take care of the baby in Chennai, a city about two hundred kilometers away, during their visit. For the sake of both the mother and child, we agreed. Almost every weekend, we traveled to the city by train to be with the baby.

On one Friday evening, as we were getting ready to go to the railway station, I heard a knock on the door. When I went to check, I was surprised to find my previous boss, who had been my first mentor in the health service sector, and his wife standing outside. He was then the head of the CSI Rainy Hospital in Chennai where I'd worked previously. Along with them was our favorite former colleague, who had driven them down. My mentor's wife said that they were traveling to Bengaluru, and all throughout the journey from Chennai, her husband had talked about visiting us. We told them that we were in a rush to catch a train, and my mentor was a little disappointed. He told us that they were planning to spend the night in our house. I felt ashamed of the state of our humble home, as I knew how comfortable their villa was. You see, when my late father had been the CEO of that hospital, our home was one of the garages for the hospital vehicles. It was later converted into a small housing unit. Sometimes when my dad's friends passed by the house, they asked, "How could you live in a house that was one of the garages of your father?" Little did they know that some of our happiest times were spent in that little cottage, and many happy memories were linked to that humble dwelling.

We quickly got the house ready for their stay while anxiously keeping an eye on the clock. After exchanging pleasantries, my mentor took me aside and said that he had come to invite me to rejoin his team as the first nonmedical junior administrative officer of the then century-old CSI Rainy Hospital. He told me that the vacancy advertisement would be placed the next week and asked me to apply. I was speechless, as the position offered better pay, and in my view, it was a step up in my career. We left them in our place and managed to catch the train. On our return trip, we also brought Abishek back with us.

I applied for the job as advised. I was amused to see that the advertisement was tailor-made to meet my qualifications. Unfortunately, I had to undergo surgery to remove a perianal hematoma, and I was recovering when the call for interview came. There was no chance of postponement, so I agreed to travel by train to attend the interview. The thought of sitting on a hard, wooden second-class bench for three hours was a nightmare. I was thinking of buying an inflated car tire tube to sit on but felt embarrassed by the thought that other curious passengers may be amused or even ask awkward questions. It was then that Rachel suggested I borrow and wear one of her sanitary napkins for the journey. I felt strange, but avoiding pain and the risk of the healing surgical wound getting infected made me accept her suggestion. So I wore one and took along a spare for the return journey. It taught me how inconvenient those things were, and I sympathized with the ladies who needed to wear one every month. The interview wasn't difficult, and soon I got the job offer letter. I was a thirty-year-old when I got that job. We moved back to Chennai.

Interestingly, throughout my career, I have been invited to new jobs or promoted to higher posts that I was not qualified for at the time of joining, barring one or two jobs that I was qualified to formally apply for. My last job was also by invitation. I confidently state that it is because of God's favor alone.

A few months after I joined, the hospital received a notice from the labor commissioner, stating that our workers had joined the communist labor union and that we were required to attend conciliation talks in his office. When my boss told me that I was to represent the hospital, I was simply flabbergasted. I had no legal training or business management qualification then. I asked him how I could be a negotiator for the management against one of the toughest labor unions in India. He said that he had faith in my abilities and knew I could do it. His confidence in me certainly did not encourage me, and I felt as though I was between the proverbial rock and a hard place.

After a few sessions of negotiations, my lack of ability to convince the other party became apparent to me. But my mentor did not give up hope. I enrolled in a post-graduate diploma in labor law to gain confidence. I had to spend a number of evenings with the legal advisor and at the university. Life became stressful, robbing me of peace. Soon some of the militant workers started making crank calls. A telephone extension was only available in the electrician's workshop, outside the staff quarters. I had the additional responsibility of ensuring that hospital bills were settled by families of patients who unfortunately passed away after the hospital's regular working hours. I was given the authority to waive part of the payment if they were poor. Hence there was no way to avoid the crank calls. I had to get up in the middle of the night to attend to the calls many times, disturbing Rachel, our child, and his nanny. I could not complain because the crank calls were anonymous. Informing the conciliation officer did not resolve the harassment. Soon the anonymous calls turned threatening. I did not want to file a police complaint, as I did not have enough faith in them taking effective action. Moreover, I had to consider the credibility and reputation of our hospital.

Between the electrician's workshop and our staff quarters, there was a large, open well barricaded by a wide three-feet-high parapet wall. Abishek was fond of playing on the long veranda shared by three housing units. The veranda was about eight feet wide and paved with black limestone called *Kadappa* stone. The well was about five feet away from the veranda. One evening, a crank caller told me that Rachel would get molested when she went shopping. I was very upset but decided not to scare her. Soon thereafter, another crank caller said, "We know where your son plays. See how close the well is to where he plays?" The message was obvious to me and needed no further explanation. I decided to quit the job immediately. But the thought of losing regular income scared me.

One of my unfulfilled wishes was to learn a musical instrument. I started learning the piano during an annual school vacation. But not having a piano at home prevented daily practice. While in Malaysia, I bought a guitar, but before I could learn, I had to return to college in India. But at least that helped my youngest brother become a skillful guitarist. I tried to learn Indian classical music, but the guru's demands were unacceptable. Over time, I realized that perhaps I didn't have a proper sense of rhythm. The only consolation was my ability to write songs. But whenever my cousin or brother scored music for the words I was inspired to write, I felt a little disappointed that I was not able to compose a song. So one day, I made an SMS prayer (more about that later): "Lord, you give me the words, but why not give me the tune as well, as you know how disappointed I am? Amen."

The evening after I received the threat to drop Abishek into the well, I went home depressed. I pulled up a folding chair and sat on the veranda outside the door, facing the well—one of the two we had bought on monthly instalments. I lit up a cigarette, as I used to smoke then, and sat there, wondering what I should do. Abishek came out and started running along the veranda. He was a quiet, skinny child with no inclination toward being aggressive. I had a cup of coffee beside my chair and, once in a while, took a sip. It was perhaps the coffee with milk and sugar that attracted an ant. I will never know.

Ants live in colonies. From our understanding, the female ants are classified as queens, soldiers, and workers, based on the roles they perform in a colony. The winged males that appear periodically move from one colony to others to participate in procreation, dying shortly after. King Solomon observed that there were no leader ants, so he advised the sluggards to observe the ants and learn. He said, "Go to the ant, you sluggard; consider its ways and be wise! It has no commander, nor overseer or ruler, yet it stores its provisions in summer and gathers its food at harvest" (Proverbs 6:6–8 NIV).

It is said that lonely ants do not survive the absence of relationships ensured by colonies for long. I don't know how true that is, but I can say that like ants, the absence of relationships can be fatal to human beings in more ways than one, especially with regard to quality of life as well as mental and emotional health.

If we realized and cherished the value of relationships before we ruined them, world peace would not be an impossibility.

The lonely ant caught the attention of Abishek. He ran from one end of the veranda to step on it. The three-year-old lifted his foot as high as it could go and came down on the ant with all the force he could muster in his skinny limbs. I was about to shout at him to stop, but I couldn't. He tried twice more, but that lonely ant crossed the veranda—all eight feet of it—without a scratch on its tiny body. The lonely ant crossing the veranda escaped. My mind compared the size of Abishek's foot and the ant. I felt that for the little black ant, it must have been like the sky falling on its head—something that frightened even the indomitable Gauls of the village of Asterix and Obelix. Before I heaved a sigh of relief, my very first song with a tune and words came into my mind, inspired by the miraculous escape of that ant. I rushed inside, picked up a notebook, and wrote it down: A Tamil gospel song called "*Sirujeevanaiyum Kanmanipol Kaappavar en Yesuve*" (meaning My Lord Jesus saves even the tiniest of creatures as though they were the apple of His eye). The rest of the lyrics were inspired by Matthew 6:25–34 (NIV):

> Therefore, I tell you do not worry about your life … Look at the birds of the air; they do not sow or reap or store away in

barns, and yet your heavenly father feeds
them … See how the flowers of the fields
grow. They do not labor or spin. Yet I
tell you that not even Solomon in all his
splendor was dressed like one of these.

Interestingly the stanzas came to my mind in reverse
order, and I wrote the lyrics as they were inspired. I have
not changed the order even today. The third stanza
was inspired by Psalms 91:7–8 (NIV): "A thousand
may fall at your side, ten thousand at your right hand,
but it will not come near you. You will only observe
with your eyes and see the punishment of the wicked."
The tune was actually a lullaby. That night, I sang the
song to Abishek before he went to sleep. He fell asleep
listening to it. I got greedy, asking for more songs with
tune in prayer, and composed a second song the very
same night.

The next day, I knew what to do. When I made the
suggestion to my boss, he said, "Be careful, *Thambi*!"
Thambi means *brother* in Tamil. He offered to send
someone with me, but I declined. He sent me in the
hospital van. The driver we all loved very much offered
to go with me, but I made him stop the van about a
couple of kilometers ahead. I told him to wait and that if
I did not return in an hour, to inform my boss. I walked
to the lonely spot where the union office was located
in a dilapidated building. Being the timid person that
I am, every step of the way, I felt like turning back and

running, but I walked on, praying every second. Once I reached the building, I climbed the stairs with shaky legs, reaching the first floor, which had an open space where a union meeting was in progress. To my shock, the tougher of the two union leaders I was familiar with was chairing the meeting. Seeing me, he was taken aback and loudly demanded to know what I was doing there. The people around him were angry laborers, and they were all glaring at me. The leader offered me a seat.

I mustered up enough courage to say, "Sir, I'm a young employee of my hospital, which has assigned me the task of representing the management. I'm an employee just like the people you represent. I'm a worker just like them, and I do my job to earn a living. Is that a crime? Even if that is a crime, why should my wife or child suffer because of me?"

He was bewildered and asked me what I was raving about. I realized that he had no idea that I was being threatened almost daily. Once he heard me out, he told me with ice in his voice, "You go home. It will never, ever happen again."

I thanked him and left. The crank calls stopped from that day. Looking back, I realized that both the ant and I were in a similar predicament, and we were both saved by the omnipotent God of the universe who cares for us. If that's not love, what is? It is that amazing love that gives speed to the tiny legs of a small creature and courage to face destructive power to a weak coward.

Nightmare Baby

"I'm seventy-five. I'm a baby!" loudly declared the older passenger.

Oh no, a boring creature across the aisle from me! That was my first thought. The one-way conversation had started when the drink trolley on the WY 102 from London to Muscat had delivered its magical brews and moved on. The man across the aisle got his drink. After the drink, he felt like lecturing. Since a mother and her daughter were seated beside him, he chose to dish out his philosophy on life to me.

He told me that he was a Canadian who had been living in Toronto for the past forty-one years. Then he scared the life out of me by loudly criticizing his faith to justify his drinking. His vocal tirade included abusive language and almost obscene gestures. To top it all, he told me that he was an Iranian Jew with an Islamic name because his father was Muslim. Imagine my shock and fear when the man became increasingly garrulous. His speech was complemented by rude gestures. I kept praying that he wouldn't end up having serious trouble, dragging me into it. I tried not to respond, but he kept tapping on my shoulder to continue the dangerous verbal dance! I even considered asking for a change of seat. But the flight was full.

Just when I thought things couldn't get any worse, he picked a quarrel with the lady seated beside him. Her daughter felt offended and reacted. In anger, he threw the airline pillow across the aisle and on the seat in front of me. Fortunately, the passenger in that seat had just gone to the toilet at the time. I thought that I would also be questioned if the lady complained. When the food trolley turned up and the meal service started, he demanded that I get him one more drink. That was the last straw. I made up my mind to complain to the flight attendant about him, but when he turned up, I couldn't bring myself to do it.

While waiting for his second drink and dinner, he told me that he was a businessman in Toronto, where he employed forty-five people. He asked me how much money was really needed to live well. He went on to say that he only kept a little for his needs and gave away eighty percent to his employees. Soon enough, I saw him making peace with his neighbor and her daughter. Well his unverifiable claim of generosity and his willingness to render an apology were the only lights in the otherwise very dark tunnel of his presence and verbal assault on the plane.

When he saw that the girl seated in front of him was served dinner first, he loudly questioned why. Hearing him, she turned around and offered him her dinner, which he gladly accepted. A few minutes later, I saw him put down the tray that she gave him and push it under her seat without touching anything. Little did I know that it was his contingency plan for a second helping. While thanking her, he reiterated, "I'm a baby at seventy-five," guffawing at his own justification of childish behavior.

Soon after dinner, he fell asleep. I thanked my lucky stars, but peace did not last long. Throughout the night, he kept getting up to meddle with his luggage in the overhead cabin; in the process, he sat on my left shoulder almost every time he bent down. That and his frequent tapping on my shoulder kept waking me up. Perhaps by tapping on my shoulder, he was attempting to tinker with the dent caused by his sitting on it. I thought I would end up walking lopsided after disembarking from the plane, resembling a mobile leaning tower of Pisa.

As the plane was descending, he removed his luggage from the overhead cabin and lined the two bags up on the floor of the aisle. After a harrowing debate, the flight attendants got him to place one of his bags back in the overhead compartment. He got up, opened the cabin, and literally threw the bag inside. He pushed one between his feet, and with a wide grin firmly pasted on his face, he acted as though he had won a battle. When the plane finally came to a stop, he was the first to stand up. He kept mumbling and grumbling until we were allowed to disembark. To my misfortune, he left after threatening me with a future meeting in Muscat.

I don't know what was going on with him, but his childish behavior made me wonder if he was a lost, lonely, and discarded human being. I thought that perhaps his tormenting legion of monsters were inside his soul and incessantly tortured him. Absence of caring, sharing relationships can give birth to such virulent inner monsters. Perhaps he was no longer able to control anyone in his family or the work place. That inability may have led to an overpowering urge to control every situation and those around him, knowing full well that such attempts were doomed. His inner monsters may have blinded him so much that he could not recognize the threats posed by his behavior.

I thought that he called himself a baby because he knew he consciously threw tantrums to seek attention and establish control over others. He represented all the complexity and vagaries of human character as well as behavior in old age, when there are no more real battles to fight; no more games to play; and sadly no loyal, understanding relationships. His aggression by choice was only an extension of his sad, frustrated, and—in his subconscious mind—futile existence. He may have been so disgusted by the sense of his aged adulthood being worthless that he chose to hide behind the persona of an innocent baby. Perhaps in his eyes, what he had become led to the regression and embracement of what he believed he had been as an innocent baby.

In other words, his loss of faith in the present made him think his imagined beginning more worthy of continued existence.

I am trying to learn something from those thoughts, as I am also a senior citizen now. Strangely I feel all right that I did not complain about him. He was my living lesson for seven hours that night. In his childish antics, I finally saw the ugly, destructive madness that could afflict us in old age if we fail to realize that anger, disappointment, and regret are human responses when loved ones let you down. A curative alternative is to remember that more often than not, people will let you down. But take up your hurt with the one true Counsellor and Comforter in prayers for healing. Moreover, learn to forgive and forget the hurt by His grace so as to restore your faith in human relationships. If we fail to have such a strong anchor in faith to sustain our sense of self-worth and dignity as well as to value meaningful relationships, bitterness will overpower us and turn us into nightmares for others. Therefore, I pray. Remind me daily, Lord, that "The silver haired head is a crown of splendor and glory; it is found in the way of righteousness" (Proverbs 16:31 AMP) and to be faithful in my relationships.

Tears in a Toilet

Having spent more than a decade in the Middle Eastern gulf region, I have come to understand the plight of the exploited and poor compatriots with a little more sensitivity and clarity. Hold on before you jump to conclusions. In a majority of cases, the exploitation starts at the country of origin. Depending on where the worker hails from, the need to go abroad could be due to an array of unfortunate reasons: abject poverty, caste, lack of educational opportunities, crop failure, being the sole bread winner of a family, serious debt burden, etc. Economic-induced suffering makes these vulnerable groups rely on ruthless agents who lie through their teeth to deceive them. Believing in tall, false promises, they arrive in wealthier countries to make a living. Only after arriving at the destination do they realize that they have accepted a raw deal and that the agents have duped both the employer and employee. Such is the nature of economic human trafficking.

These vulnerable victims borrow heavily to pay the so-called employment agents. Many cannot return even if they want to, as their passports are confiscated upon arrival, and for others, going back is never an option because of the loans to be repaid, for instance, redeeming a small piece of farm land that may have been mortgaged to pay the extortionate fees charged by such a devious employment agent is impossible without large amounts of money. They are forced to stay on and work, dehumanized with no sign of hope. Some victims suffer a worse fate, as they are deceived by unscrupulous agents who disappear with the promised job after taking their money. Such people resort to suicide. Politicians generally turn a blind eye to these victims, as there is no personal financial gain in lobbying for their welfare. Being a witness to the plight of these unfortunate and never-recognized souls has opened my eyes.

As I was growing up, I never had any lengthy conversation with my father, because I was simply in awe of the man who, in his prime, towered above ordinary mortals like me. He was, above all, a generous giver, never counting cost. This gradually pushed him from prosperity to mere survival. Today's sermon in church was about generous giving based on second Corinthians chapter eight. The preacher confirmed some of my own thinking about giving, but he added insights that reminded me of my father's practice. Quoting from the Bible, the preacher told us that the poor congregation in the Macedonian church deemed it a privilege to give, as they insisted on giving despite their own extreme poverty. That nicely summed up my dad's attitude toward giving. The world may have considered my dad an unwise person because he gave until he himself became poor. But for me, he left a legacy for which I thank God and certainly my dad, my hero. He kept driving his philosophy of giving into his children's heads, citing Proverbs 19:17 (NIV): "Whoever is kind to the poor lends to the Lord, and he will reward them for what they have done." Not that he was an angel but he tried to be humane and human in the best sense of those words when it came to generosity. Dad not only gave to the poor but to anyone in need—so much so that he once fed an entire circus troupe and their animals for three days because the cashier had absconded with the collected revenue, and they were stranded in our town. My mother supported him; although, she tried to make him aware of the future once in a while.

Astonishingly once he was down, I never heard him complain about his life, nor did I hear him express regret about what he had done for others. I'm not that kind of a giver, but I do try to remember his instruction to put into practice generous giving. In short, my dad's philosophy of life could be summed up with the words of the Bible: "Do nothing out of selfish ambition or vain conceit. Rather, in humility value others above yourselves, not looking to your own interests but each of you to the interests of the others" (Philippians 2:3–4 NIV). He practiced that philosophy while I struggle to try.

Thanks to that legacy of Dad's and the enhanced awareness of the expatriate worker's plight, I at least extend a smile to the workers in malls and other public places. Sometimes I greet and chat with them, and on some occasions, I give them a little gift, hoping it will ease their burdens during the day. They respond by helping me park my car, advising me where I should keep my belongings, and showing concern for my health and my family's wellbeing.

Being a diabetic, one of the places I regularly visit in any mall is the toilet. The folks serving there invariably recognize me and clean up the toilet for me by spraying an extra dose of disinfectant and freshener. I hope it is not to prevent me from infecting anyone! Once a gentleman worker didn't like the idea of me carrying shopping bags into the toilet space. He sternly advised me to keep the bags on a platform outside, saying that no one would bother to walk away with those bags. I did not listen to him and kept the bags on the ledge inside the toilet, but later on, I realized that he was only giving me sensible advice. How he recognized that I am from his home state in India is puzzling, because he addressed me in my mother tongue.

Over time, I made it a point to chat with the man whenever I visited that particular set of restrooms, and he made it a point to choose a toilet and clean it specifically for my use during those visits. This generous service had been going on for some months. Weekends in Muscat are Fridays and Saturdays, so our church worship is on Fridays. On that particular Friday, on my way back from church, I visited the toilet where he was posted. I saw a worker with a tonsured head cleaning a particular stall, and I thought it was him. I waited for him to finish cleaning, and as he stood up, I recognized him. I was about to ask him if he had fulfilled a vow to his god and tonsured his head. Then I saw his clean shaven face and realized that there must have been a death in the family.

He saw my expression of concern and said, "My father!" Shocked, I asked him when. He said, "Last Friday," while trying to hold back the tears that began to flow.

I could not say a word as I tried to share his pain. Eventually I asked him, "Did you go?"

He stuttered and replied, "My passport is not with me, and I wasn't granted leave!" I couldn't console him. I didn't know how, except to hope that he would find comfort in my tears.

Responsible fathers are lonely creatures; they have to balance the role of a caring parent with that of a police officer or, more appropriately, responsible steward of the family. So it is tough for them to express their love in words for fear of their children taking too much liberty, which may eventually lead them up a wrong path. Some fathers have to go far away to ensure a comfortable life for their children. It is only through perseverance in prayer for the family that they sustain their own lives. Dad had to do that for more than a decade. My father was a remarkable human being. At his funeral, a cousin stood by his casket and remarked, "If it were not for him, we wouldn't be where we are!" His brother seconded that. I hope my epitaph will be at least half as close to such a sentiment!

On the Threshold

As the vehicle turned into the gateway, I felt excited and cautious, even apprehensive. A new job in a different institution always makes the butterflies in my stomach hyperactive. After a brief meeting with the president, I headed toward the HR office like a robot—not like Arnold Schwarzenegger in *Terminator*, more like WALL E before he met EVE. The manager offered me a seat and then started his briefing.

"Your working hours, sir, are 8:30–5:30, with an hour lunch break from Sundays to Thursdays, and on Saturday, it is 8:30–2:00." I nodded in acknowledgement, and he continued, "You can meet the provost and then come back here for a presentation on HR policies."

I couldn't help but think of my former colleagues in various HR departments. Like a sleepwalker, I went through the routine and headed to my office. "In the seven months since my interview, they have put together such a sparkling new wing!" I exclaimed to myself. The board above the high arch at the entrance informed me that it was the Information and Learning Center Building. When I had first visited the campus, it contained only the library and an empty stretch of land behind it. But now it was a sprawling floor with offices, discussion rooms, and a multimedia lab. The board outside my office said distance education department. Memories of Manipal rushed in, crowding my mind. I recalled former associates, colleagues, and friends who helped me serve there. I noticed two things: the offices for the boss and his secretary were of equal dimensions—that was a first for me—and all the walls and furniture were white. "How am I going to keep the place spotless?" I asked myself nevertheless remembering that white was the preferred color of the health professions.

I remembered the HR briefing: 1,300 staff. A flood of questions popped up in my mind: Will I ever get to know ten percent of them? With my incapacity for remembering names and other important things, how many times am I going to offend people or get insulted by them for attributing wrong names? I wished I had Ash's photographic memory!

Are these thoughts and memories of people I have worked with in the past trying to tell me something? I wondered. I remembered that the last anecdote I wrote before leaving my previous job was about a farewell party organized by former colleagues elsewhere. I had then remembered names and faces of people I had lost touch with, perhaps forever. Why were these memories so heavy and painful? Why was it so difficult to settle down in a new place without remembering the people you had closely interacted with in the past?

Leaving a job is not just about leaving entities, organizations, and institutions. It is more about leaving relationships, and that is why there is pain when we remember the people who were part of our past. We may have had misunderstandings with them, even quarrels that ruined relationships, but once you move away from the places where those relationships were born, nurtured, and grown, you see their unique value and the value of your unique relationship with them more clearly and objectively. That is why there is also apprehension about the relationships that are about to begin in the new place. There will be differences of opinion and misunderstandings in this new workplace too. Therefore, I started my new journey with a prayer: "Lord, help me not to repeat the mistakes of the past. Teach me to value the relationships that you allowed to bloom in the places where I served. May those whom I worked with forgive me for the pain I may have caused, and let them know that I see their true value now. Therefore, I thank you for those with whom I have served and those with whom you have called me to serve in this new place. Prepare me for this new journey and the new relationships. Give me the wisdom and sensitivity to value and appreciate those relationships. Guide me throughout this journey. Amen."

Limitless

"What is man, that you are mindful of him?" (Psalm 8:6 NIV). That is a question from King David that I often ask God in the context of my average but not necessarily ordinary life—a life full of challenges, falls, pains, and astounding blessings. David asked that question while marveling at the grandeur of God's creation. I ask that question every time some life situations throw a curveball or a googly.

In July of last year, I downloaded my *Adhar* card (national identity card) and brought it along, as my passport was due to expire in August of 2020. The threat of COVID-19 was looming large over the horizon by early 2020. Because I was running out of pages and had only eight quarters across two pages left for immigration stamps, I contacted the agency responsible for processing passports in January of 2020. When the lady who took my call heard that my Adhar card was printed in July of 2019, she told me that its validity had expired, as the printout could not be older than six months before the date of application. I needed to get a new printout of my Adhar card to submit with my passport renewal application. I was flummoxed to say the least. The Adhar card was necessary if you had to change your permanent address. I had to make a weekend trip to India in February since one-time passwords (OTP) for printing the card were only sent to the phone number registered in the original application, and the Indian SIM card for that number was with me in Oman. The possibility of India initiating a lockdown worried me. But the trip also gave me an opportunity to visit my mother, who was ill at the time. So I went to India on February 6, got the Adhar card printed, and came back.

Due to laziness, I did not get back to the agency that processed passport renewal for Indians in Oman. I had to pay for it with worry and anxiety. Muscat was placed under a partial lockdown by April 10, which was extended twice. As it got closer to July, my anxiety multiplied. In June, when I contacted the agency, they told me they would get back with me, but no one got back. Nobody answered the phone as well. So I went to their office one day, and I was told to get an appointment. I told them that no one was answering my calls, but a gentleman there told me to try in the afternoons. Finally, I got through one afternoon, and they gave me an appointment to go there on June 29 before five in the afternoon. I told them, "I can't fill out the online form, print it, and sign it, as my printer scanner is outdated, and I'm unable to get the toner for it after work because of the lockdown period starting at six in the evening." They said that was not a problem.

I worried some more because of what happens to those who do not join the popular political bandwagon in India these days. I had already been threatened twice in my life—once in person more than a decade ago because I'm a Christian and more recently for my political views expressed on social media. During the face-to-face message sent through a friend who also happened to be a member of a very powerful political association masquerading as a social organization, I simply quoted the words of Apostle Paul: "For to me to live is Christ, and to die is gain" (Philippians 1:21 KJV).

My faith is quite shaky during any crisis, and in trials imagined or real, I pray, quoting Mark 9:24 (KJV): "Lord, I believe, but help thou mine unbelief." All of you familiar with my Facebook posts know that I'm never politically correct. So my trepidation grew as days passed. I was wondering what would happen if there were trick questions in the online application form.

Another reason for my anxiety was that decades ago, I made a serious mistake with my name when I went to collect my secondary school leaving certificate (SSLC). Those days, it was in a red-colored book that grades were entered in by hand. The teacher in charge of grade entry asked me if my name was Jesudasan. I felt that my first name was not fashionable, so I said it was Jesudhas. The teacher looked at me and asked,

"Are you sure? Your admission form says otherwise. Your father wrote Jesudasan." Since I was ashamed to repeat the lie, I simply nodded my head. He said, "Be careful. This is a record for life." I felt like telling him it was Jesudasan, but you know how it is. Once you lie, you can't have the courage to accept that you had lied. As a result, my academic records have one version of my name, and my passport has the original name with a special entry for the alias in an older passport. Like it or not, I have to carry that older passport as well whenever I travel. This is my first public confession on the matter. Because of that one error, I have had to provide extra documentary evidence for jobs, visas, etc. throughout my life. I have also lied repeatedly, pinning the blame on an imaginary clerical error—although never in writing.

On June 29, I reached the agency's office—a stone's throw away from my office—like a man confronting a horde of imagined demons, as that's what they were. I entered the office with three other people, only to be promptly told by a peon to get out as it was in vogue in any Indian bureaucratic office or allied service provider on contract. I stood my ground while the other three guys scurried outside, terrified. When I said I worked for the Ministry of Health, it was the peon's turn to retreat. I pointed to my name on the clipboard list of those who were scheduled to visit at the time. He backed out and asked me to proceed to counter one.

Counter one was managed by a middle-aged lady

who was very courteous. I gave her my documents and told her that the renewal application had to be processed by her office, as I could not fill out and print one. She reassured me and agreed to fill it out for me. Then she looked at my passport and Adhar card. I was prepared for tough questions, but she asked, "From Chennai in Tamilnadu to Manipal in Karnataka?" So as true to my old-age-engendered habit, I gave her a long story on how that happened. She listened patiently to most of the rambling and quietly replied, "I'm from Udupi" On hearing that, all my trepidation disappeared. Manipal is a city in the Udupi district. The proximity of our places of residence created an instant bond of camaraderie. I remembered David's question and thanked God. What was the probability of someone from Udupi attending on an anxious, old applicant from Manipal over thousands of kilometers across a sea? Two perfect strangers meeting at that time, on that day, with one desperately needing reassurance.

She did all that was needed to be done, but there was one final hurdle. She asked me for my local address, and I couldn't remember it correctly. So I gave her the office address. But she needed the postbox number to complete the form. I did not have it. After some struggle, she decided to complete the form by mentioning the landmark nearest my office, the Khoula hospital. I thanked her profusely and asked when I would get the passport. She answered, "In ten days."

I'm stupid enough to look at gift horses in their

mouths, so I retorted, "Last time it took only three days."

Forgiving my audacity, she politely replied, "You know the situation now, sir. The embassy is very busy."

I said, "I understand," then thanked her again and left, making a mental note to inform the security guards at the college gate after July 1.

A week later, on my way back from office on a Thursday, the day before the weekend in Oman, I realized that I had not yet informed the security guards. I decided to inform them first thing on Sunday morning. But on Friday afternoon, I received a call from an unknown local number, asking me who and where I was. To my utter amazement, the gentleman on the phone said he had my new passport to deliver. I was shocked. I wondered how it could be, on a Friday, a weekend holiday. He asked me if anyone would be at the college. I told him only the security guards, but I hadn't informed them. Then I told him I lived in Al Khoud and could drive down and meet him. He mentioned a location I did not know. Then he told me he lived in Al Hail, a neighboring area of Al Khoud, and could hand over the passport at the Shell petrol station that was just past the Caledonian college. That was the route I took to office daily to avoid peak hour traffic. Again my mind recalled David's question: "What is man that you are mindful of him?" What was the probability of the embassy's courier living almost walking distance from my residence and delivering my passport on a Friday?

When I collected the passport, I offered to show some identification document. He took one look at me and said there was no need of that.

I'm a worrier, despite the fact that I have seen miracle after miracle in life. Never once has God denied His tender mercies to me; they have always been limitless. It is sad that despite His faithfulness to me, my faith gets shaken now and then. So I continue to pray, "Lord, I believe, but help thou mine unbelief."

Fragrant Friendship

Leather and Lather, one of my favorite perfume shops, moved from the Avenues Mall to the City Center (CC) in Muscat this year. I was also happy to see that Lush is about to reopen in the CC. I have been a regular customer of both shops for the past few years. Those of you who know me may remember that one of my major weaknesses is an obsession with scents and perfumes. That's why, even in our small garden in India, I have planted different types of fragrant plants and vines as well as five trees that bear fragrant blooms.

Even when my personal economy was akin to the pre-1991 national economy of India, I used to scrape the barrel to buy fragrant hair cream and perfumes. I'm sure many of my friends had silently suffered from my liberal splash of perfumes on my clothes and pulse points. Life in Malaysia made me enjoy a variety of perfumes, and the personal economic boom in Oman only enhanced my indulgence. One of my biggest problems is what to do with half-empty bottles of perfumes, colognes, lotions, etc. when I leave Muscat.

I keep promising myself that I won't buy anymore and try to use up what I have. Several weeks ago, Leather and Lather sent me a discount sale offer. I resisted it until today, September 29, 2021. The shop had three very smart, young men serving customers, and one of them always liked speaking with me. More than once in the past, I have had to politely excuse myself to avoid irritating other waiting customers.

One of the reasons why I go to that particular shop is because I'm partial to British and European perfumers. Today I decided to make a courtesy call. This young man was alone, serving a lady customer. Once he saw me, he almost forgot to attend to her. I went around, testing the new brands. While she was looking at some product, he quickly approached me and recommended two Miller Harris perfumes made in London. I liked both but settled for the bergamot-vetiver combo.

After the lady customer left, I reminded him about the discount offer I had received several weeks ago. He promptly guaranteed that he would give me the best price. I started my career as a relief salesman for Brooke Bond India, so I knew that usually all the sweet talking was to promote business. But sometimes you also end up finding friendship as an outcome of the business interactions.

When I told him about my plans to retire, he got excited and asked me dozens of questions about future plans. He advised me to go on a world tour. I politely told him that I couldn't afford one. Then he asked me if I had travelled abroad. When I nodded, he questioned me on the countries I had travelled to and my experiences there. Good thing no other customer turned up. When I told him what I was planning to do after retirement, he was visibly impressed, like a hero-worshipping son.

As usual, he forgot to check out my purchases. Finally, but reluctantly, I pointed to the box, and he enthusiastically billed the product. I was stunned to see that he had given me a discount of thirty Omani rials (OMR), roughly equal to seventy-seven US dollars (six thousand INR). The current price of one hundred milliliters of that perfume in India is 12,800 INR. He kept up the chatter, appreciating my future plans almost to my embarrassment. As I finally took leave, he came around the counter, put a hand on my shoulder, and wished me well. For some unknown reason, I felt moved and blessed him. Fragrant relationships may be momentary, but the scent of such relationships stay with you, bringing a smile to your face whenever you remember.

About twenty-eight years ago, during a crisis, I was inspired to write a little song, remembering the incidence of the woman breaking the alabaster jar to apply perfume to the feet of Jesus in Mark 14:3 (KJV). Here is the song:

> My life is broken.
> Praise God; praise my Lord.

My eyes are filled with tears.
Praise God; praise my Lord.
My heart lies bleeding within, and
the pain is so severe.
But there's a fragrance of love
pervading everywhere.
I have been broken.
Yes, I have been broken
to release the Christ in me.

There is no greater gift in life than the genuine love of people: friends, family, and even a sales person. I thank God for my fragrant friend and continue to bless him in prayer.

A Heart of Gold

I heard about the Mall of Muscat and its aquarium, so I visited. It was one of the biggest I had seen. I spent more than two hours exploring and taking photos to share on Facebook. When I went there, my car was dirty because of the rain the previous evening. I parked the Nissan Patrol in one of the open parking lots on the mall grounds. When I returned to the car after the visit, I found it washed and one of the windshield wipers extended. I was surprised because I did not ask for the car to be washed nor saw anyone with a mobile car washing unit. I looked around for a couple of minutes or so. Not finding any of the parking area attendants, I left.

On my way back from work on Thursday, I stopped at the CC, which was closer to my home. I found a guy who was washing cars and paid for my car to be washed. Because of my regular interaction with them, they respond to me with kindness. After shopping, another young worker approached me when I reached my car. He had washed my car at the parking lot a few times before. He was younger than my sons. He said, "I saw your car at the Mall of Muscat, but I did not see you. It was dirty, and I felt bad, so I washed it."

I asked, "Who paid for it? I did not see you!"

With a smile on his face, he replied, "I did"

I was amazed by his kindness and paid him back. I have seen much ingratitude in my life. I have also not been grateful on some occasions. I wondered if I would have bothered to wash his car if our roles had been reversed. He may have seen my car among hundreds purely by chance. But to stop and wash it voluntarily, adding to his workload, and then paying for it proved that he had a heart of gold. It was entirely possible that he may not have been posted at the CC again nor knew who I was and where I lived. It was also possible that being an expatriate, I could have left the country in the intervening period.

I have always considered Jesus's statement, "The poor you will always have with you" (Matthew 26:11 NIV), in a different context. This young man's act of kindness taught me something new. The poor know how to respond with unconditional love if you treat them with kindness, dignity, and respect, for they are certainly wealthier in terms of the riches of heaven.

Forty-Three to Friern Barnet

Christina, my niece, said goodbye and left at six. I watched her taxi disappear into traffic from the entrance of the hotel. I marveled at the transformation of her personality, which was now an amalgamation of maturity, courage, and confidence, so I thanked God for His blessings upon her. Since I did not feel like going back to my room, I wandered around Islington, taking some photos. When we played monopoly as children, I always thought it was pronounced Ai-lington, but in reality, it is Islington. I had dinner at a Thai restaurant. When I returned to the hotel, I decided to use the gift coupon for a free drink. Thereafter I went to bed. But right after I changed clothes to settle down for the night, I decided to check the directions for Colney Hatch Lane, where I was to locate a publisher the next day. Google search gave me three transport options. I decided to take bus forty-three to Friern Barnet, notwithstanding the fact that the thirty-one intervening stops from Islington to my destination would be a matter of concern with regard to the duration of travel.

After a hearty breakfast in the morning, I walked to bus stop J at Islington. There was one other gentleman seated at the bus stop. I sat on the other end of the bench. Looking at the poster beside me, I decided to take a selfie with it in the background. Hearing the camera shutter, the other gentleman demanded, "Hey, are you taking my picture?"

I was startled by his aggressive tone of voice. *What audacity? Who does he think he is?* I thought. So I said, "No," bluntly and showed him the photo I had taken.

He apologized, realizing that I was annoyed. I was so irritated that it made me glad to see him take a different bus. Once I had boarded my bus, I found a window seat. Most of the folk taking the bus were elderly, like me. Some looked like centenarians. A few young people were also there. The passengers included representatives of various human races, with the majority being white.

A couple of stops past St. Mary's Church and St. Mary Magdalene Church, an old lady a few rows ahead of me started talking loudly on the phone. Her voice was drenched in hopelessness and helplessness, teetering on the very edge of irreversible desperation. She spoke about her need to take painkillers to tolerate diverse aches and persistent agony, her psychological trauma, and her utter loneliness. Then she told the person on the other end that she would share more information during Wednesday's visit. She was so loud that everyone on the bus heard her sad tale. Just before she ended the call, she stopped midsentence to apologize for being so loud to her neighbor seated beside her. I could see a dark-skinned hand reach out and gently pat her on her shoulder, indicating it was all right. I caught a glimpse of silvery hair as well. The lady on the phone responded, "Thank you, darling!" Compassion, the great leveler, neutralized color differences in an instant.

I wondered if, in that single moment, one old person transferred some of her own strength to another lonely old neighbor by the power of her human touch to combat the suffering that old age brings. That's what it looked like to old me—an angelic touch of mutual consolation from one person on the way out to another in the same boat … I mean bus!

A Father's Wish

As a school boy, I was able to outperform many of my peers in academic and extracurricular activities but not in sports. Therefore, I was considered a nerd and treated like one. Almost everyone who was familiar with my academic achievements wanted me to become a physician like my father. I was influenced by their constant encouragement. The school went so far as to predict that I would rank first in Tamilnadu's SSLC public examinations.

Early adolescence made me an emotional wreck, and I could not fulfill that dream. However, I was first in English in the North Arcot District and was awarded a cash prize by one of the teachers. My younger brother saw it as a golden opportunity to celebrate, because he received it on my behalf. I was away at college, reading at the pre-university level at the time. When I came home for a short vacation, he told me that he had received the prize and had enjoyed spending it.

While all others advised me to become a medical doctor, my late father—who was a specialist in chest medicine, particularly tuberculosis—advised me to get the real doctorate. It was decades later that I understood he was referring to the title doctor of philosophy, the highest academic degree. My father probably felt that it was not right to equate the title associated with the highest academic degree to undergraduate and postgraduate medical education. But the world appears to feel otherwise.

Once my father came back from meeting one of his friends—a police official—he told us how impressive it was to see the then district collector, a female Indian administrative service officer in her twenties, command respect from such a senior police official on her visit to our town. He then looked at me and told me, "Join the civil services or get the real doctorate." Well like all good and obedient sons, I did not bother to pursue either goal.

I did not do well at the undergraduate level, due to many attractions, distractions, and attractions that became distractions. But I woke up in time to get a master of arts in philosophy. Thereafter, I joined Brooke Bond India as a relief salesman—a job that I gave up prematurely. It took three years of odd jobs, a lot of wasted time, and a second degree in medical record science to get back on track. It also took six years of service in mission hospitals to reach my first Brooke Bond India salary.

I joined the Oman College of Health Sciences in October 2019. Yesterday, October 22, I was told that I would not be paid salary for the current month, since my employment was yet to be confirmed by the government ministry concerned. Anticipating the need for money, I approached the people who owed me. One returned the call to apologize, but the other repeatedly ignored my messages. For some reason, I was not unduly perturbed.

My college officials told me that the payroll window at the ministry closed every tenth day of each month, and I would probably get my salary by the end of November of 2019. One even told me that for some people, it took about three months from the date of joining. I decided to visit the official I had first met at the Ministry of Health on October 1, my first day at the new job.

In the morning, before leaving home, I requested a pastor and my sister to pray. I had asked others to pray the previous evening. As I drove to the ministry, I caught myself singing the Tamil version of the hymn "Oh! Jesus I have promised." Once I reached the recruitment office, I could not find the gentleman, and I was told that he may or may not report for work. I decided to wait for him. Soon enough, he turned up and greeted me. He was a very kind Omani gentleman, probably older than me.

He searched for my file on the shelves next to his table but eventually found it open on his table right in front of him. He checked the papers and found a document with Arabic writing on it. He told me to wait while he walked up to another colleague to discuss matters. Yesterday I was told on the phone that the delay was due to finance ministry processes. He had not replied when I had asked him about that. But when he came back with the paper, he told me that he had received the necessary approvals just then. I asked him if it was an issue with the finance ministry. He said, "No. No, it is about approvals from the Ministry of Civil Services. Your visa will be processed in three working days!" I thanked God but wondered why the approval had arrived only while I was waiting there and not in the twenty-one days before.

As I walked back to my car, it hit me. I had not planned to fulfill my father's wish to get a PhD, but I had ended up getting one because someone else who was due to go to Manipal had turned down the offer. I went there as a substitute. My father could not attend the convocation, but I managed to show him a video clip of that event.

Those who witnessed my open defense were surprised by the external examiner's remark that it was a path-breaking PhD. I neither deserved that compliment nor aspired for it. There was a time in life when I was proud of my achievements and even arrogant. It was only later in life that I learned humility after God dealt body blows to my attitude. Whenever tempted to show off, I remind myself of the biblical instruction: "Humble yourselves, therefore, under God's mighty hand, that he may lift you up in due time" (1 Peter 5:6 NIV).

Today I officially joined the civil services of a foreign government at the age of sixty-two years and ten months. If I remember right, the age limit to appear for the civil services examination in India was twenty-six during my college days. I had no plan to get a PhD, or join the civil services to fulfill my father's wish, yet the heavenly Father chose to fulfill my earthly father's wish. I'm glad that He, in His grace and mercy, chose to do that through me! And I'm also glad that my father lived to see the PhD. I wish he was here today!

True Faith Must Walk the Talk

My life has been filled with many financial crises. Despite holding high-paying jobs for more than twenty-one years, I must confess that I have not been a responsible steward of my personal finances. I often forgot the lesson in the book of Proverbs: "He becometh poor that dealeth with a slack hand: but the hand of the diligent maketh rich." (Proverbs 10:4 KJV). My slack hand was due to multiple complex reasons. Fifteen years in Oman made everyone think that I must have been rolling in wealth. But those closest friends who were witnesses to our struggles during the mission hospital days knew my real predicament. I won't say I'm poor, because it is an insult to my God, who has always opened His eternal storehouse to meet my family's needs. As a family, we were not poor by any stretch of the imagination, but we could have done better and avoided the financial insecurities that we sometimes felt.

A debt-ridden and extraordinarily commitment-filled

life has kept me working until now, and that is why I have not been able to retire and do the things that I want to do. I know it is hard to believe, but that's my reality. I must confess that years of indoctrination about doing one's duty at all costs makes me feel like a wretched victim oftentimes and increases my sense of guilt for feeling so. Such negative thoughts occur when people do not realize that I could not pay fatherly attention to my children while they were growing up. I had to stay separated from my family over those fifteen years while others had that blessing. But fortunately for me, such thoughts don't get me down or overwhelm me, as I surrender them in prayer daily. Hence my soul sings with gratitude to God all the time.

But there are other reasons that I am reluctant to confess. The very first day I drove my sports sedan to the college, many colleagues were surprised. Some were happy that I had bought a head turner. When someone told my boss, I believe he said, "He has a lifestyle problem." He was not off the mark. Another conveniently ignored cause of slackness that contributed to my financial woes was the genetically hyperactive taste buds that generations of my family are notorious for. I must accept that living beyond means comes to me naturally—not that I regret my well-lived life.

God has always rewarded me unexpectedly. Whenever that happens, I remember my dad's favorite quotation about giving to the poor and lending to the Lord. However, whenever there is a new financial crisis, my wavering faith makes me forget that lesson. Since I send most of my salary to my family in India, retaining just about enough for me in Muscat, Oman, I was close to running out of funds when my salary was delayed. My old boss, some family members, and a trusted friend graciously helped me manage one month. I found it extremely hard to ask people for financial help. This situation was temporary, and I knew I would sort out all the pending payments soon enough. But to be safe and due to my lack of faith, I started making contingency plans.

Yesterday in church, my nephew and his wife, a young couple asked me if I had gotten my salary, since I had told them about it earlier. I replied in the negative. After church, I went to the Avenues Mall to window shop. Over a cup of coffee, I was wondering who to ask for help in case there was further delay. I hoped for some friends residing close to that mall to walk in and see me. I told myself that if any such friend walked in, I'd seek his or her help.

Throughout my life, I have experienced my unsaid prayers being answered. I received a call from the young couple, asking if I was still in the mall. I said, "Yes!" They told me to wait, drove all the way back to where I was, and gave me a surprise gift. When I assured them that I would pay them back immediately after getting my salary, they refused to accept, saying it was simply a gift of love. There was absolutely no need for them to do what they did, and I prayed for God's choicest blessings upon them.

A young Bangladeshi man comes to clean my house every week. I enjoy talking to him, as he always talks about the importance of value-centered living. He also keeps praising me for my negligible acts of kindness. I feel that no worker should be denied his due once he or she has performed the tasks assigned. So as usual, I paid his salary on time last month.

Today he turned up, and the conversation included the topic of my delayed salary. He stopped sweeping and told me there were very few people in this world who think of the needs of others like I do. I felt great and thanked him.

It was then that he said, "I have been sitting and thinking about borrowing fifty OMR ($129) from someone. But no one will give me that much." I was about to say that if I got my salary I'd give it to him, but he continued, "You see, sir, I have been thinking about you, and I told myself that if someone loaned that amount, I could gift it to you!"

I was speechless. My salary was many times greater than his, and I knew from past conversations that he was never paid his wages—approximately one hundred OMR per month—on time by his employers. He got paid once in three or four months. He has never once asked me for more than what I usually pay him. But I have never seen him worried or anxious. I also knew that he was the only bread winner in his family, consisting of dependent parents, siblings, wife, and children. The only thing I did for him was pray for him and his family every day. I never once thought about his needs as he had mine.

I realized how weak my faith was compared to his. He gave me examples of how God has miraculously helped him on many occasions. He smiled and told me that since I was a good person, God would take care of me. In conclusion, he said, "When a good person falls, God lifts him up in unexpected ways, but when a wicked one falls, God makes him learn a lesson; even allows him to suffer until he corrects his ways!"

Thanks to his words and actions, I do not worry about the future as much as I did before. I'm learning to lean on God in faith, for He has never once let me down in any crisis. It is so easy to lose sight of the promises of divine support that sustain us through every situation. I hope that like this young man, I will soon learn to rest on God's resources rather than my own. I pray that his faith in action will be rewarded immeasurably from the eternal riches of God! His name is Ameen, and I say Amen.

SMS Prayers

As I groggily returned to the land of the living, I heard the crows first and thought, *Oh no! Not another day.* The murderous chorus of crows at dawn was akin to a team of football players singing their national anthem, and it declared the start of my daily game of life and death. My troubles had started while I was preparing to do well on the final university examinations and win the Naomi Carmen gold medal for the best outgoing student in the medical record science program. It started with fever, and I went to the staff and student clinic almost daily. I started on a liquid diet and took the tests the doctor ordered. The results showed no abnormality. But almost every night, I had chills and was taken to the casualty by fellow hostel mates, as our hostel was in the medical college hospital compound. My hostel mates were preparing for their exams as well, but they selflessly helped me. The doctor put me on antibiotics just to be safe. God only knows why I did not return to my home 155 kilometers away even after the final exam, but I continued to stay in the hostel.

On that fateful evening, a few days after my exams, an Anglo-Indian friend wanted to have a beer in the evening. He asked me to go with him. Once he got his beer, he offered me one, but I declined. As he was having a drink, I stood there, listening to him. Suddenly I felt as though someone had punched a hole inside my guts with a rifle shot. I broke out in a cold sweat and couldn't talk for a few seconds. I told my friend that something terrible had happened and that I needed to get back to the hostel. Every step I took was a nightmare. The strange thing was that neither he nor I thought of walking into the emergency wing, which we had to cross on our way to the hostel. Once I reached the hostel, I went to the toilet but felt no relief. Then I tried to lie down on the bed, but that did not help either. The excruciating pain made me toss and turn. I did not want to disturb friends, who had already wasted their examination preparation time to take me to the hospital several times.

However, past midnight I could not take it anymore. I don't know how I managed to get dressed. I reached Sharath's or Alex's room and knocked. When the door opened, I collapsed on the two, who were sleeping on the floor after a late-night group study session. Jag, Ebby, Raj, Sam and others lifted me. One of them ran all the way to the casualty in his pajamas to bring a wheelchair. I couldn't wait. I ignored the pleas to stay and wait for the wheelchair. I dragged myself with the aim of reaching the casualty on my own steam but collapsed again near the tennis court. Friends eventually rushed me to the casualty. The duty doctors had called for surgery unit one to examine me, as they were the first on call. The intern on duty profusely apologized for not doing enough during my previous visits. I feebly told him that it was not his fault. Someone had told me that the then vice principal was a man of prayer. I wanted his unit, surgery unit three, to look after me.

My world turned upside down. An emergency laparotomy was done, and when I woke up, I was given forty-eight hours to live. Peritonitis had set in. After the removal of the drain, the ten sutures were closed in the ward while I was partially conscious. Needless to say, my screams brought the roof down. The diagnosis was a single perforation at the ileocecal junction. Enteric fever? But no significant abnormal values showed up in lab tests to confirm enteric fever. The doctors hit me with antibiotics and, toward the end, with an antimalarial drug as well. Nothing worked. Strangely it is thirty-three years later, at a conference in Oman, that I got the opportunity to meet and thank the surgeon who had performed the emergency laparotomy

My mother and sister flew back from Malaysia. My aunts, brother, and cousins arrived. My father-in-law-to-be had alerted them. I was out of it all. Thirteen days of agony followed the emergency surgery, but many people intervened to declare God's decisions over my life. My classmate Thomas's mother ensured that I was kept in A ward when my family decided to move me to a private ward. She convinced everyone that A ward had the best nurses. Until that point, I thought of nursing as a secondary profession, because my father was a physician. If it weren't for the nurses of A ward, I wouldn't be writing this. Chitra, a nurse, along with my cousin Prabhu tried to ambulate me every day. They bore my entire weight on their shoulders. I felt sorry for them as they invariably gasped for breath and broke out in sweat. Jolly, Rachel, Shirley, Caroline, and the student nurses made sure that I was looked after. I owe my life to them. Never did I realize that decades later I would end up running an undergraduate nursing program as dean of a health sciences college.

I counted every drop of the IV fluids that was pumped into me. Young medical interns were constantly in attendance. Some of them took the trouble to answer my anxious questions with patience. My hands became so swollen that they resembled those of Popeye, the sailor man. Padankatti aunty and her friend were the only ones who could draw blood from them. Eventually a decision was taken to do a venous cut down. Worried about complications from the procedure, Caroline came to me and said that she would try to locate a vein on my foot to start the IV fluids. She apologized for the pain she would cause. Considering her determination, I agreed. She inserted the needle first under the skin of my left foot and then the right to search for a suitable vein. She was perspiring. I held on silently, tolerating the agony. Finally, she gave up and ran to the nurses' waiting room. I could hear her weep inconsolably, and the senior nurse reprimanding her.

My bowels refused to restart. Test feeds were rejected. My eyesight began to fail. A few days before I heard the crows, I saw an arc of green fluid go over my mother's head and hit the window. It was like the scene from the *Exorcist*. I told my mother to look out, only to realize that the projectile was from my mouth. It was released with such pressure that the Ryle's nasal feed tube flew out. Piyu was on duty, and he wanted to reinsert the tube. I pleaded with him to let go. Strangely he agreed after a consultation over the phone. Two days of purging started, and it was so much that the ward had to borrow draw sheets from the neighboring ward. Nurses on night duty were served tea early in the morning. On the horrible day that I had uncontrollable purging, the student nurse Jolly brought her cup of tea and fed me, saying I must be exhausted. I looked at her tired face, kind eyes, and caring smile. I felt emotionally moved by gratitude as the smell of my feces on her hands overpowered the smell of the disinfectants she had used to wash them.

Around noon the next day, Dr. Joe, the vice principal, called my mother outside the ward. I overheard him tell her to send for my father, as they could not do anything further for me. When she returned to my bedside, I looked at my mother and knew that she had also given up hope. I told her to remove the pillow from under my head and just place the tiny Gideon's New Testament there. I must confess that there was no discernible inner prompting to do that. I just felt like asking her to. That's the day I fell asleep with peace in my heart. Just before I slept, I prayed my shortest prayer in a crisis. I prayed for my mother, sister, and all those who had looked after me. My only worry was Rachel, as she was engaged to marry me at the time, so I prayed for her strength and future. Finally, just before I fell asleep I prayed my first SMS prayer: "If You have a purpose for my life, spare it, Lord; otherwise, let my loved ones not suffer anymore because of me."

I woke up to see the exhausted face of my mother, who had nodded off beside the bed. Not just the riotous cawing of the murder of crows but also the gentle touch of the student nurse had woken me up. As she was about to place the thermometer in my mouth, I knew that my troubles were over. She took the temperature, and her eyes opened wide when she looked at the thermometer. You see, the major problem for the doctors was the high fever that wouldn't subside even after my bowel movements had restarted. I smiled at the student nurse and asked her if it was normal. She looked bewildered. She ran and got Shirley, the senior nurse on duty. Shirley brought a new thermometer and checked; it was normal. I don't know who was happier. I think it was a close thing between my mother, the nurses, and me. Two days later, I was wheeled out of the ward. My mother and I went to collect the discharge summary from Dr. Joe's office a week later. After signing the document and handing it to my mother, he looked at me and said, "I don't know how you survived. God must have a purpose for your life."

I still don't know if I have fulfilled that purpose. To tell you the truth, I'm not sure I know the purpose. I constantly worry about the souls that I may have lost rather than the ones I may have saved. I also do not know how to pray. I keep repeating the same petitions over and over again for a number of people and those who ask me for prayers. Rachel has a much longer list of people to pray for. But interestingly, I can recall every SMS prayer that has been answered. These are usually the ones that I do not speak aloud. These SMS prayers are not even consciously made sometimes, whether they're about travel abroad, the desire for a favorite ice-cream, mundane requests, or miracle-seeking petitions.

Rachel once asked me, "Why does God love you so much that He grants whatever you ask for?"

My answer has always been simple. "I don't know!"

Two years ago I contracted dengue. Since I read a lot about the disease, it only contributed to my anxiety, just like my knowledge of microbiology and pharmacology kept increasing my anxiety and fear in 1984. My probing questions annoyed one trainee doctor so much that she blurted out, "This is why we should limit the information we give to patients!"

But that kind of knowledge eventually got me the Naomi Carmen gold medal. Nowadays ill-informed media channels complicate matters by discussing every inconsequential detail of any infectious disease. During my dengue episode I prayed an SMS prayer almost every day: "Lord, let me not die in sin or alone; let me complete my duty to others."

When COVID-19 reached our shores with a bang, I got a PCR test done after one of my colleagues tested positive. The next day, when I was told that the result was positive, one question kept popping up in my mind: Why now? I sent prayer requests to family and friends. I felt lonely but pretended to be brave. While in home quarantine, one of my colleagues called to enquire after my health. She was surprised that I was laughing and joking on the phone. I was not vaccinated at the time. I just had throat irritation, nasal congestion, and an upset tummy. I can't figure out why I had started snacking on expensive macadamia nuts and Brazil nuts—both immunity boosters—about two weeks before the PCR test. My doctor put me on azithromycin, and I started taking vitamins C and D and Neurobion. I do not know if these things worked. Literature says that they do not.

I did worry about writing a will and getting help printing and signing the document. I asked the caretaker to keep an extra key to my house, as I did not want anyone to suffer if I died in my sleep. More importantly, I wanted my body to be found before decomposition. I'm a sixty-four-year-old diabetic on BP medication with a rare high-risk blood subgroup of A1 Negative, and I live alone. As today marks the end of COVID-19 for me, I can tell you that my current SMS prayer has also been answered. "Lord, let me not die alone in a foreign land. Let me not die in sin; there is much to be done." This morning I read about King David, who was a past master of the art of praying, and I agree with him that "The Lord has heard my cry for mercy; the Lord accepts my prayer" (Psalms 6:9 N IV).

I do not know why the Creator of the universe loves me so much. David cried, "Save me because of your unfailing love" (Psalms 6:4 NIV). I'm not even a speck of dust in comparison, but one thing I know is that the Lord loves me and accepts my SMS prayers. I have one more SMS: "Lord, please reveal Your purpose for my life. If you have already revealed, make me aware, and help me fulfill that faithfully. Amen and Amen."

Practice Humility
Doctors (PHD)

The academic degree doctor of philosophy (PhD)
originated in the Muslim world in the ninth century to
distinguish between the highest scholarly achievement
and other doctorates awarded in some academic
disciplines. It moved to Europe and the Americas later.
The first European PhD was awarded in Paris in the
twelfth century. Today the value of the degree is greatly
compromised by PhDs awarded to callous academics
who carry out poor quality research and those purchasing
commercialized titles. However, a quality PhD is still
considered the hallmark of academic scholarship.

I never imagined that I would earn a PhD and
become an academic; although, it was my father's dream
for me. It was purely accidental that I eventually wound
up with a doctorate. It took four years of research studies
for me to get a PhD. Soon after I was awarded the
doctorate, a colleague and friend who believed I had
bought the degree asked if I could get him one. So much

for my credibility. Some of my old acquaintances insist on addressing me as mister, reminding me that in their view, I didn't deserve the title of doctor.

Once a former colleague who reported to me went around saying that since I am Indian with a PhD from an Indian university, my doctorate was not equal to his Australian master's degree. He even engineered a student strike, using that as an argument. In the early days, I used to get upset by such reactions, thinking that my hard-earned academic qualification was being discredited.

It all started when I was advised to apply for a national fellowship by the leaders of what was to become one of my alma maters. They somehow felt that I had potential after a brief meeting in Delhi. It was a surprise meeting, because my boss had suddenly invited me when I was hardly prepared. After reaching the venue, I realized my organization was exploring a collaboration with the university. Following that meeting, the university leadership sent me the application and prospectus; although, I was completely unaware of the project details.

Eventually I attended the selection interview at the university. But I lost out to a smart, young lady who had a research proposal addressing gender issues. The next year, I tried again. The selection interview turned out to be a nightmare—the toughest interview that I have ever faced. I heard that there were twenty-five candidates from all over India competing for that single seat, but I do not know the actual number.

When I came out after meeting with the selection panel, I was perspiring so much that a peon felt sorry and offered me coffee. Seeing my plight, one competitor who was waiting to face the panel asked, "How was it?"

I replied, "I feel as though I was molested by a gang." To be truthful, I mentioned the *r-word* synonymous with molested. I went home and said the same to my wife.

The next morning, the news leaked that I had been selected. When my boss returned from abroad, he congratulated me and, to my sheer amazement, said that I had topped the selection list. The research study changed the course of my life dramatically. Even before I received the original certificate four years later, I was appointed as assistant dean in a college abroad. My thesis made some waves among peers. I felt grateful to God first and those who had encouraged me. My parents, who were alive then, felt proud, I'm sure.

I no longer care about how people address me, mainly because I have learned that I am who I am in the sight of God. Secondly, age-wise, I'm on borrowed time. An academic title, however hard earned, will never define me. No human being will ever know me for what or who I am. I'm Tommy to some; JF to others; Thomas; Tom to my siblings, peers, and my wife; and Dada to my children. I was Thoma to my late father and Thamu to my grandmother.

I'm at a stage in life where my only concern is who I am to my creator. I'll feel truly rewarded only when or if He considers me worthy and awards me eternal life in His presence. In other words, if he counts me among the progeny of the father of the righteous, Abram—who, in the sight of God, was Abraham (Genesis 17:5 KJV). Or if that is far too arrogantly ambitious, I wish to be counted among the progeny of the once-stumbling, impulsive, prone-to-failure, and emotional Simon, the fisherman who, in the sight of Jesus, was Peter the rock (Matthew 16:18 KJV).

Stranger Angels

I washed banana skins in soap before peeling and eating the fruit. I carried several types of sanitizers and used them everywhere. I showered before going out and after returning. I wore masks that matched my office wear. The SARS-CoV-2 was having a great laugh at my paranoia, I guess.

On March 29, 2021—the day my young colleague walked into the office and announced that she was feeling unwell and going home early—I knew trouble was on the way. Just that morning, we had shared coffee. The previous day, we had used the same laptop for a presentation. The next day, she called and said that her PCR was positive and advised me to test. I rushed to the nearest test center and got it done. The following day, the virus came home happily and called me loser.

My health profile told me to write a will, but my faith said hold on. The torment started then. I put up a brave front and laughed when people called. But down inside, I worried about all my loved ones. I'm no stranger to a death bed and have been living on borrowed time since 1984. After the confirmation of COVID-19, I felt abandoned, mostly by the people I had expected to show concern and care.

The thing about isolation is that it shows you how important relationships are. I longed for comforting and caring words of encouragement from those I thought would spontaneously reach out to me. Well that was a bummer. Family worried, but strangers stepped in and stood in the gap—those whom I did not personally know from church, particularly a saintly lady; a former colleague I had quarreled with, who was a stranger to me because he was agnostic; and the Muslim Bangladeshi building caretaker.

I sent prayer requests and received encouraging words from priests. But there was a deafening silence from those I trusted and relied on, except for a courtesy text or two. God was teaching me something new. Three Omani colleagues in particular kept me going; they kept in touch with me every day. One Omani and a Jordanian called to check on me. They made me fight the battle by God's grace.

The virus had the last laugh; it left me with post-COVID-19 depression. Everything looked worthless. Life itself felt devoid of meaning and purpose. A stranger stepped in—the young, female Omani colleague. Forgetting cultural and gender differences, she asked me to walk with her along the beach road— even though she was fasting during Ramadan. I did that for a few days. We walked eight kilometers daily.

Realizing that it helped me recover slowly, I continued to walk alone. My mood changed gradually but surely. Her presence during the walks helped me take my mind off the worrying thoughts that plagued my mind.

Last week, after my mother-in-law passed away, COVID-19 visited our home again. I thought my young son would heal faster than me, but that was not so. He needed hospitalization. Strangers stepped in to help, like his Hindu college mate who had come to our home for vacation; he stayed on to be the backbone of the family, like a son. Abishek's friend, a Hindu physician I had never met before, took our boy under his care and looked after him. Last night, both Rachel and I were broken in every sense of the word. We wept together, telling each other that God would not let our son down. The accuser saw the opportunity to torment me, piling guilt upon guilt. I received scriptural advice, reassuring texts, and prayer support messages. I was truly a man who could not even pray. But I held on to the certainty that the God of tender mercies, who I worship, would not let our son and our family down. We continued to hold on to that assurance.

This morning, I went to a hospital that provides twenty-four-hour services to get pre-travel testing done. When I stepped into the emergency ward after registration, a stranger stepped out. Despite the mask she was wearing, I knew there was a radiant smile behind it. I told her why I needed the PCR. She took a long look at me, and I felt the kindness overflowing from her heart. She even told a fellow staff how difficult it must be for me. Then she gently took the nasal swab and asked me if I was all right. I asked her for her name, and she cheerfully said Rakhi. Nurses are called sisters, and here was my Rakhi sister. *Raksha Bhandan*, the Indian festival based on a historical event, symbolizes men adopting unrelated women as their sisters, promising to protect them. It is popularly called *Rakhi*. I thanked sister Rakhi for her kindness and blessed her.

Just before leaving for India, I got the news that our son was doing well under medical care. I texted him and received positive feedback. To be better prepared for follow-up care and considering Rachel's health profile, I decided to get ahold of an oxygen concentrator to take home. To my disappointment, people were paying exorbitant prices and sending them to India. I was told that there would be none in stock until May 10. My colleague tried but couldn't find one. I did not give up. I googled the suppliers' list and called several, but the response was the same: none in stock!

Then I checked the least promising web link for a dealership. I was told that they had some in stock and were selling at regular price. I immediately proceeded to collect one. One of the other retailers called me and asked if I would share the information if I managed to find someone who had them in stock, as they had many desperate people waiting. I reached the location, but finding the dealership was difficult, as I did not know it had moved to the second floor of a new building.

Eventually I found it. As I was about to locate the elevator, I received another body blow—a text from home that said Rachel had fainted and fallen down. Fortunately, our Hindu maid Divya was there to help out. She refused to stop visiting to help although she was cautioned about the risks of infection to her and her family. After exchanging messages and getting confirmation that Rachel was awake and resting, I reached the office of the dealership.

I knocked, and when the door opened, I was confused by the expressions on the faces of the gentleman who opened the door and the one standing behind him. After a pregnant pause, they welcomed me in. I saw a carton by the side of the door and assumed that it was probably the oxygen concentrator. I told them why I needed it. I could not stop giving them all the details, including the news of Rachel fainting. The gentleman in charge asked his office boy to demonstrate the machine to me. After the demo, I went to pay the bill, but he told me that they only accepted cash, as their credit card reader was out of order. He felt bad about making me go get the cash but directed me to the nearest ATM machine. I drove like a robot on valium, almost meeting with an accident on the way to the ATM.

I returned to the dealership with the money and settled the bill. I was also worried about my sugar levels going south, as it was well past my regular meal time. It was then that the seller refused to give me the receipt. He told me to sit down on the only chair that had a prayer mat hanging on its back. I told him I was in a hurry, but he refused to hand over the receipt. I could not think straight. Part of my mind was suspecting a con job, while the remaining parts were coping with the news from home as well as the fear of a hypoglycemic episode. When I reluctantly sat down, he asked me something in Arabic. I managed to guess that he had asked if I was fasting during Ramadan. I replied in the negative and told him that I was not Muslim. I noticed the office boy lurking near the entrance to the office. The gentleman told the boy to get me something to eat and drink. I was shocked and asked him how I could eat in the presence of people who were fasting.

He said, "You need food now, and we cannot let you go."

I had not said a word about my diabetes to him or his office boy, but they had somehow recognized that I was in trouble. Soon the office boy brought in some snacks and tea. I could not thank them enough for their life saving hospitality. When the office boy brought the concentrator down and helped me load it in my car, I gave him a tip. He refused to accept it, but I insisted and put it in his shirt pocket.

He told me, "Sir, when we opened the door, we were both shocked to see the expression of agony on your face. So when you left to get the cash, the manager and I said a prayer for you and decided to feed you."

I could not say thank you or God bless you without

a sob choking my throat. As I drove off, I saw him standing by the roadside and watching my car.

COVID-19 was disastrous for millions. Some of us were fortunate to get out of it, but we lost friends. A number of people lost their loved ones. During that period of affliction, some of us were not only spared but had been taught lessons that we were previously blind to.

For me personally, it was a time to realize that all the assumed or imagined differences that made someone a stranger were not worth considering anymore. Religion, gender, and nationalities did not stand in the way of those strangers who wholeheartedly cared for me. They were simply the good Samaritans when I was a wounded Jew and those with whom I identified myself had no time for me, much like the Pharisee and the Levite. The self-righteous, hyper religious, and theologians may accuse me of misquoting the Bible, but believe me, I no longer judge. I choose to follow the teaching of Jesus whole heartedly, not to judge, and that is certainly not out of the fear of being judged (Matthew 7:1 KJV). I do not judge because these strangers—Agnostic, Hindu, Muslim, Omani, Jordanian, Pakistani, Indian, Bangladeshi, women, and men—that God sent to me during my and my family's COVID-19 nightmare have given a whole new meaning to my understanding of "There is neither Jew nor Gentile, neither slave nor free, nor is there male and female, for you are all one in Christ Jesus" (Galatians 3:28 NIV).

Bruised Reeds

My early success in my career and the resulting recognition and admiration of peers had a negative impact on me. The consequences of such impact are usually long lasting, and they scar your soul. But like cardiac ablation—where tiny scars are made to restore proper rhythm of one's heart—such scarring, however painful, can restore you to a state of harmony with the God-given principles of life.

Since early childhood, I have been familiar with the verse "A bruised reed he will not break, and a smoldering wick he will not snuff out. In faithfulness he will bring forth justice" (Isaiah 42:3 NIV). I recall an aunt often quoting that verse to counsel worried relatives. My meeting with Anthony helped me understand that verse as the very essence of God's justice. Our system of justice must take into account bruised reeds and smoldering wicks. We must remain sensitive to those.

Somewhere along my decade-long journey in the healing ministry of the Church, I had lost that sensitivity. I became a self-certified expert on healing and wholeness and an outstanding event manager to promote knowledge of holistic healing. I can imagine how painfully amusing it must have been for some of my family members, peers, friends, and other victims of my self-certification. In reality, I had lost the sensitivity to distinguish between arrogance and confidence. I was prepared to take on any challenge head on, imagined or otherwise. Chest thumping became the order of the day.

I was asked to organize a disaster management workshop at an idyllic venue on the east coast, closer to Mahabalipuram. The budget-resort-like venue was established by one of the oldest colleges in Chennai. When a colleague and I reached the venue, my first task was to see if the board and lodging were to my own inflated standards. You see, you cannot lord it over people unless you act superior to them, even if you are really an inferior human being.

It was at the venue that I met the temporary caretaker, Anthony. He was a nervous young man standing in for the manager, who was on vacation. Since I was from a medical organization, Anthony kept addressing me as doctor; although, I was not a member of the exclusive country club that was the medical profession. My criticism affected him strangely. Whenever I raised a query, he trembled like a leaf caught in a storm. My patience soon ran out.

One evening after sunset, Anthony invited us to catch crabs on the beach. We went along with him and his coworkers. We watched them chase elusive crabs and catch a few. Anthony's colleagues treated him like a child. They always ran back to show him what they had caught, which provoked hearty laughter. I found it extremely funny. On the way back, Anthony was excited and cheerful; that was probably the only time he was not nervous in my presence.

The dining area was not as clean as I wanted, and the same glasses were used to serve water as well as tea. Although the glasses were washed and reused every time, I could always find fault with the washing. While I was waiting for a phone call in the dining area one night, the opportunity to express my displeasure presented itself. It was after all the workshop participants had left the dining hall following dinner. My colleague was also there, waiting for his turn to call his family. We did not have cell phones those days. Anthony was having his dinner with other workers. They were all very young, hardly in their twenties.

My colleague and I approached their table, and I must confess that the dinner was simple but delicious. But who cares? It was my golden opportunity to deliver a lecture on health and hygiene. I also had to impress all of those gathered there—particularly my colleague from a different city—with my knowledge, sense of discipline, and problem-solving ability. Anthony patiently listened to my lecture.

It was the strident ringing of the telephone that irritatingly to me but mercifully to the audience, put an end to the drivel I was dishing out. As I got up to take the phone call, I noticed that Anthony had stopped eating; I did not know when. On the way back to our rooms, my colleague politely chided me, and said, "You could have been gentler." I decided to make amends to Anthony as best as I could.

Early in the morning, I noticed a visibly worried Anthony supervising the cleaning of the dining area. At lunch, we were given separate, larger glasses for water. I congratulated myself and generously gave an imaginary pat of appreciation on my ego. Anthony kept glancing at me nervously. I thought he was probably a recovering drug addict. I may not have been a medical doctor, but I had become an expert due to a decade-long service in a medical organization. By mere observation, I could diagnose underlying causes of nervousness!

On the final day, after the conclusion of the workshop, I met Anthony to settle our bills. I apologized to him for the late-night lecture but thanked him for addressing my demands.

He replied nervously that he had learned a lot from me. "I rely on God for everything these days, doctor. So that night, before going to bed, I read the Bible and prayed, 'Lord, I'm so weak and inadequate. I do not know how to do my job. Please help me.' I felt better after that."

Although I felt sorry for him, I gave in to my unforgivable insensitivity. To satisfy my expectation of Anthony confirming my diagnosis, I asked, "Anthony, what is wrong with you? Why are you so nervous?"

He mumbled in response, "Doctor, I'm being treated for schizophrenia."

I was stunned and speechless. His reply was like a slap on my face. No, more like God wielding His sword of justice; cutting through my ego; destroying all that was proud and arrogant within me; removing the ugly, calloused insensitivity; and creating scars of healing to restore harmony within my soul. It was an ego ablation, restoring the proper rhythm of value-centered living.

I will always remember Anthony. Meeting him was the milestone that taught me never to judge anyone blindly or lord it over someone. I wish I could go back and remove the pain I caused to Anthony—a bruised reed. But the scars left by our meeting remind me that God used him to bruise me in ways that made me a better human being. Therefore, I continue to pray, "Lord, please let me never again break a bruised reed nor snuff out a smoldering wick. Amen"

Bibliography

Thomas, J. F. "A Bruised Reed" *Christian Medical Journal of India* 11, no. 4 (October–November 1996): 5.

http://biblehub.com/
https://www.biblestudytools.com/
https://www.youversion.com/
https://open.life.church/partners/youversion
https://en.wikipedia.org/wiki/Ant
https://www.linkedin.com/pulse/8-attributes-ant-we-can-implement-business-sneha-mehta#:~:text=Ants%20live%20in%20colonies%20consisting,carries%20out%20their%20tasks%20faithfully.
https://www.theclassroom.com/history-phd-degree-5257288.html

Printed in the United States
by Baker & Taylor Publisher Services